KT-166-566

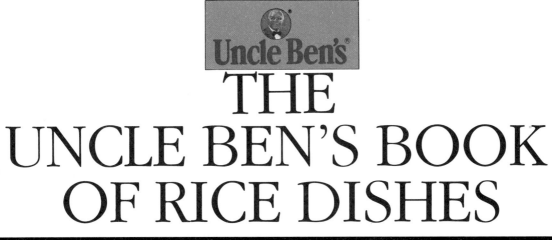

THE
UNCLE BEN'S BOOK
OF RICE DISHES

Colour Library Books

INTRODUCTION

Although rice has been grown in China since 2800 B.C., it was not until the Middle Ages that it was imported into Britain, where it was destined exclusively for the tables of the rich. Medieval rice recipes were for luxurious dishes, flavoured with almond milk and either saffron or sugar and served on special occasions. By the 17th century, rice was in wider use and milk puddings were flavoured with spices and included eggs and breadcrumbs.

In the 19th century, as the British Empire grew, so too did the taste for the exotic cooking of the colonies and the Victorians enjoyed such savoury rice-based dishes as curry and kedgeree. Yet it was only with the increasing popularity of Eastern food, in the second half of this century, that rice became firmly established in the British diet.

There are over 7,000 recorded varieties of rice. Short grain rice is grown mainly in Europe and the Far East and is traditionally used for milk puddings. Most medium grain rice in Britain comes from Italy and is used for risottos and croquettes. Long grain rice is generally used in savoury dishes and most of that sold in Britain comes from America.

Uncle Ben's rice uses only the top 5% of the crop and is, therefore, of the highest quality. Thorough processing, using a method invented and patented by Uncle Ben's Inc. in 1943, ensures that the grains retain much of their vitamin and mineral content and remain separate after cooking, giving the 'perfect fluffy grains every time', for which Uncle Ben's rice is famous throughout the world.

Uncle Ben's name has been synonymous with high quality since the early days of American rice growing. The original Uncle Ben was a Texan rice farmer, known to local millers for always delivering the best quality rice. His name became legendary and, long after his death, growers would claim that their rice was 'as good as Uncle Ben's'.

In the late 1940s, Gordon L. Harwell, the first president of Converted Rice Inc., predecessor of Uncle Ben's Inc., and his partner were dining at their favourite restaurant and discussing their marketing strategy for bringing to the American consumer the same high quality rice that they had supplied exclusively to the Armed Forces during World War II.

Searching for a suitable name, Gordon Harwell remembered the legendary Uncle Ben. So the partners decided to call their product Uncle Ben's rice, knowing that it would do justice to the reputation for high quality established by the original Uncle Ben.

Easy to store and cook, Uncle Ben's rice, whether you choose ordinary long grain or wholegrain, has an important role to play in a balanced diet, as it contains fibre, minerals, vitamins, protein and carbohydrates. And every carton carries the Uncle Ben's guarantee – perfect results every time, whoever does the cooking!

Photography by Peter Barry
Recipes Prepared and Styled by Bridgeen Deery and Wendy Devenish
Designed by Dick Richardson

CLB 2024
This edition published 1990
© 1989 Colour Library Books Ltd., Godalming, Surrey.
Printed in Belgium by Casterman.
All rights reserved.
ISBN 0 86283 764 2

SWEETCORN, RICE AND CRAB SOUP

SERVES 6

A simple, yet authentic, dish, which will liven up any dinner party.

15g/¹/₂oz butter
2 spring onions, chopped
850ml/1¹/₂ pints chicken stock
75g/3oz Uncle Ben's Wholegrain rice
1 x 198g/7oz can sweetcorn kernels, drained
1 x 175g/6oz can crabmeat, drained
2 tbsps cornflour
2 tbsps dry sherry
Salt and pepper, to taste

---

1. Melt the butter in a pan, add the onion and cook without browning, until soft.

STEP 1

2. Add the stock and the rice and simmer gently for 20 minutes, or until the rice is just tender.

3. Add the sweetcorn kernels and the crabmeat.

STEP 3

4. Blend together the cornflour and the sherry and pour into the soup.

STEP 4

5. Cook for a few minutes, until it has boiled and is slightly thickened.

6. Season to taste. Serve immediately.

Cook's Notes

[t] TIME: Preparation takes about 5 minutes. Cooking takes about 30 minutes.

[O] SERVING IDEAS: This dish makes an ideal starter to a stir-fried Chinese main course. Serve with soy sauce to taste.

[!] WATCHPOINT: The soup is intended to be of a thinnish consistency, so do not boil vigorously to thicken, as this will spoil the crabmeat.

WILD RICE PÂTÉ

SERVES 10

A fibre-filled and exciting alternative to traditionally flavoured pâtés, this can be served as part of a hearty meal.

6-8 rashers streaky bacon, rind and bone removed
75g/3oz Uncle Ben's Long grain and wild rice
15g/¹/₂oz Uncle Ben's seasoning mix, from sachet in rice packet
340g/12oz pork, minced
100g/4oz pig's liver, minced
1 medium onion, finely chopped
1 garlic clove, crushed
1 tsp mixed herbs
225g/8oz spinach, frozen or fresh, cooked and drained
1 egg, beaten
2 bay leaves (optional)
Lettuce, parsley and lemon twists, to garnish

---

1. Preheat oven to 180°C/350°F/Gas Mark 4. Lightly grease a 1kg/2lb loaf tin. Line the tin with greaseproof paper.

2. Arrange the bay leaves, if using, face down on the base of the tin and cover with the bacon strips. Set aside.

3. Cook rice with seasoning, according to the instructions on the packet. Drain.

4. Mix together the pork, liver, onion, garlic and herbs. Put half this mixture into the prepared tin and press into an even layer.

5. Cover with the spinach.

6. Stir the egg into the rice and pile on top of the spinach, to form an even layer. Press down well.

STEP 6

7. Cover rice with remaining meat mixture, pressing down well.

8. Cover the loaf tin with foil. Stand in a roasting tin one quarter filled with water.

STEP 8

9. Bake the pâté in the preheated oven for 2 hours.

10. Remove tin from the oven and from the waterbath. Place a weight on top, leave to cool and then refrigerate.

11. To serve, turn out of the tin and serve with hot toast or salad.

Cook's Notes

⏱ TIME: Preparation takes about 30-40 minutes, including cooking the rice. Cooking takes about 2 hours, plus about 2 hours cooling time.

❓ VARIATION: Increase or decrease the amount of garlic, according to taste.

BACON AND AVOCADO STARTER

SERVES 2

Sophisticated and tasty, this appetiser can be rustled up in minutes, even by the complete novice.

---

1 x 227g/8oz can Uncle Ben's 3 Minute
    Wholegrain or Long grain rice
8 rashers streaky bacon, rind and bone removed
1 ripe avocado pear
1 tbsp lemon juice
4 spring onions, finely chopped
25g/1oz walnuts, chopped
4 tbsps French dressing

---

1. Cook the rice, as instructed on the can. Cool.

2. Grill the bacon until crisp, cool, then crumble, using a rolling pin.

STEP 2

3. Peel and chop the avocado and mix with the lemon juice, to prevent discolouration.

STEP 3

4. Mix together the rice, spring onions, avocado, walnuts and bacon. Stir in the French dressing.

STEP 4

5. Serve, well chilled, in individual serving dishes.

Cook's Notes

🔁 TIME: Cooking the rice and the bacon takes about 30 minutes, plus up to 1 hour cooling time. Preparing and assembling the dish takes about 15 minutes, plus further chilling time.

❓ VARIATION: Add a little garlic purée to the dressing, if desired, or use Thousand Island dressing, instead of the French dressing.

⭕ SERVING IDEAS: Garnish with slices of lemon and parsley sprigs.

RUSSIAN FISH PIE

SERVES 4

This rich and savoury Slavonic pie is worthy of a truly indulgent evening.

Shortcrust Pastry
300g/10oz plain flour
150g/5oz butter
Pinch salt
Water, to mix

Court-bouillon
450ml/³/₄ pint cold water
1 onion, peeled and stuck with 6 cloves
1 bouquet garni
1 carrot
1 glass dry white wine

Filling
600g/1lb 4oz monkfish fillets
Salt and freshly ground black pepper
40g/1¹/₂oz butter
150g/5oz Uncle Ben's Wholegrain rice
1 large onion, chopped
450ml/³/₄ pint chicken stock
200g/7oz smoked salmon, thinly sliced
180ml/6 fl oz double cream
Fresh dill and lemon slices, to garnish

1. In a large mixing bowl, mix together the flour and salt and rub in the butter, until the mixture resembles fine breadcrumbs.

2. Make a well in the centre and add enough water to mix to a firm dough. Chill the dough for at least 30 minutes.

3. Put the 450ml/³/₄ pint water into a saucepan, along with the onion, bouquet garni, carrot and white wine. Bring to the boil, then simmer for 20 minutes.

4. Remove the pan from the heat, strain and reserve the liquid. Discard the vegetables.

5. Put the monkfish fillets into a shallow pan and pour over the prepared court-bouillon. Season with salt and pepper and poach the fish over a gentle heat for 15 minutes. Remove the fish fillets and leave to cool.

6. Melt the 40g/1¹/₂oz butter in a large saucepan. Stir in the rice and the chopped onion. Fry gently until the onion and the rice have just turned translucent.

7. Pour the chicken stock over the onion and rice, season well and simmer, stirring occasionally, until all the liquid has been absorbed. Allow to cool.

8. Wrap the slices of smoked salmon carefully around the monkfish fillets.

9. When the rice is cool, stir the cream into it carefully, mixing well to blend thoroughly. Adjust the seasoning, if necessary.

10. Lightly grease a deep sided cake tin, or flan ring. Preheat the oven to 200°C/400°F/Gas Mark 6.

11. Roll out two thirds of the pastry and use to line the base and the sides of the tin carefully.

12. Put half of the rice mixture into the bottom of the lined tin. Arrange the fish parcels carefully on top of the rice mixture. Cover the fish fillets with the remaining rice mixture.

13. Roll out the remaining pastry to make a lid. Cover the pie with this, sealing the edges with a little milk or water.

14. Make a couple of slits in the middle of the pie lid, to allow the steam to escape, and decorate with pastry shapes, if desired.

15. Glaze the top of the pie with a little milk or beaten egg and bake for 35 minutes, or until the pastry is golden brown. Serve hot, as a main course, garnished with the dill and the lemon slices.

Cook's Notes

⏱ TIME: Preparation takes about 45 minutes. The pie takes a further 35 minutes to cook.

⃞ SERVING IDEAS: Serve with lightly cooked, green vegetables and piped potato.

? VARIATION: Use fresh, home-made chicken stock, if available.

MOROCCAN SALAD

SERVES 6-8

Simple, yet sophisticated, this crunchy salad is good enough to be eaten either as a side salad or as a main meal.

225g/8oz Uncle Ben's Wholegrain rice
4 tbsps French dressing
1 small Webb or round lettuce, washed
175g/6oz cooked chicken, diced
4 tbsps thick, set yogurt
1 tbsp turmeric
2 tbsps chopped walnuts
3-4 carrots, grated
2 red apples, cored and diced, soaked in lemon
    juice
1 large or 2 small green peppers, seeded and
    chopped
1 orange, peeled and sliced
Chopped chives

1. Cook the rice according to the instructions on the packet.

2. Drain the rice and toss it in the French dressing. Set aside to cool.

3. Line a salad platter with lettuce.

4. Mix the chicken with the yogurt, turmeric and walnuts, until the turmeric is evenly blended.

STEP 4

5. Arrange the ingredients in lines across the top of the lettuce: grated carrot, rice, apple, chicken sprinkled with chives, peppers and orange slices. Chill well, before serving.

STEP 2

Cook's Notes

🕐 TIME: Cooking the rice takes about 20 minutes. Preparation takes about 25 minutes, plus about 1 hour chilling time.

❓ VARIATION: Use Thousand Island or Blue Cheese dressing, instead of the French dressing.

HOT CHICKEN LIVER SALAD

SERVES 4-5

More than a snack, this quick and tangy dish is delicious, as well as nutritious.

100ml/4 fl oz water
1 small cauliflower, cut into small florets
2 courgettes, sliced
1 x 227g/8oz can Uncle Ben's 3 Minute
    Wholegrain or Long grain rice
40g/1½oz butter
225g/8oz chicken livers
2 tomatoes, skinned, seeded and cut into strips
2 tsps Worcestershire sauce
4 drops Tabasco sauce
Salt and pepper

1. Pour the water into a saucepan and bring to the boil. Add cauliflower and courgettes, cover and simmer for 4-5 minutes.

2. Add the rice and cook for a further 3 minutes, or until water has been absorbed.

STEP 2

3. Melt 15g/½oz of the butter in a small frying pan, add the chicken livers and cook gently for about 5 minutes. The livers should still be pink inside.

STEP 3

4. Remove chicken livers and add to the rice mixture with the tomatoes. Mix together thoroughly, but carefully.

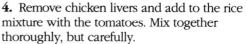

STEP 4

5. In the frying pan, melt the remaining butter with the Worcestershire sauce, Tabasco, salt and pepper. Pour this over the hot rice salad and serve immediately.

Cook's Notes

⏱ TIME: Preparation takes about 15 minutes. Cooking takes about 25 minutes.

❓ VARIATIONS: The tomatoes could be replaced by 1 red pepper, which has been cored, seeded, sliced and sautéed for 5 minutes with the chicken livers.

SWISS RICE SALAD

SERVES 6-8

You don't need to be in Switzerland to enjoy the delights of this savoury, main course salad with its fine, cheesy flavour.

225g/8oz Uncle Ben's Long grain rice
150ml/¼ pint French dressing
100g/4oz ham
100g/4oz Gruyère or Cheddar cheese, diced
40g/1½oz black olives, stoned and sliced
100g/4oz green pepper, seeded and sliced
50g/2oz salami, diced
2 spring onions, thinly sliced
1 tomato, skinned, seeded and chopped

---

1. Cook the rice, as directed on the packet.

2. Drain the rice and stir in the French dressing. Leave to cool.

STEP 2

3. Cut the ham into strips about 1.25cmx2.5cm/ ½ inch x 1 inch.

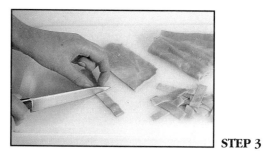

STEP 3

4. Stir the ham strips into the rice, together with the remaining ingredients. Mix together well. Chill the salad well, before serving.

STEP 4

Cook's Notes

⌛ TIME: The rice takes about 20 minutes to cook, plus cooling time. Preparing and assembling the salad takes about 20 minutes, plus chilling time.

◻ SERVING IDEAS: This dish is also suitable as a starter or as part of a buffet or picnic.

❓ VARIATION: Use chopped shallots, instead of the spring onions. Substitute red or yellow peppers for the green pepper.

PORK WITH APPLE RICE

SERVES 6

The sweet succulence of pork chops, with this unusual accompaniment, is guaranteed to whet the appetite of any guest.

---

6 pork chops, 1.25 cm/½ inch thick
2 tbsps vegetable oil
1 medium onion, cut into ½cm/¼ inch wedges
250ml/8 fl oz apple juice
250ml/8 fl oz water
225g/8oz Uncle Ben's Wholegrain rice
50g/2oz raisins
¼ tsp cinnamon
Salt
1 eating apple, sliced
Parsley, to garnish

---

1. Grill the chops and set aside, keeping them warm until required.

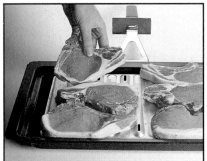

STEP 1

2. Meanwhile, heat the oil in a pan and fry the onion, until tender.

STEP 2

3. Add the apple juice and water and bring to the boil.

4. Stir in the rice, raisins, cinnamon and salt. Cover and cook for 15 minutes.

5. Add sliced apple and continue cooking, until the water has been absorbed, approximately 5 minutes.

STEP 5

6. Garnish the apple rice with parsley, if desired, and serve with the pork chops.

Cook's Notes

TIME: Preparation takes about 5 minutes. Cooking takes about 15 minutes for the chops and 20 minutes for the rice.

PREPARATION: Once sliced, put the apples in cold water, with a little lemon juice added, to prevent discolouration.

VARIATION: For a stronger flavour, use 500ml/16 fl oz apple juice to cook the rice and omit the water.

LEMON VEAL CHOPS WITH HERBED RICE

SERVES 4

For a special meal, why not try this delicate blend of lemon-flavoured chops, with a mouthwatering rice accompaniment?

600ml/1 pint water
2 chicken stock cubes
225g/8oz Uncle Ben's Long grain rice
2 onions, coarsely chopped
3 garlic cloves, crushed
1 tsp oregano
1 tsp basil
½ green pepper, seeded and chopped
4 x 100g/4oz veal chops, about 1.25cm/½ inch thick
Pinch cayenne pepper
6 tbsps dry white wine
1 lemon, thinly sliced
4 tsps chopped parsley
Freshly ground pepper, to taste
Vegetable oil, for frying

1. Bring the water and 1 stock cube to the boil in a saucepan.

2. Stir in the rice, onion, garlic, oregano and basil.

3. Cover tightly and simmer for 20 minutes, adding the green pepper after 10 minutes.

STEP 3

4. While the rice is cooking, season the veal chops with cayenne pepper.

STEP 4

5. Heat the oil in a large, non-stick frying pan, add the chops and seal them quickly on both sides.

STEP 5

6. Reduce heat. Add 6 tbsps water, the wine and the remaining chicken stock cube.

7. Arrange lemon slices on top of the chops. Cover and cook over a low heat, until meat is tender, about 15 minutes.

8. Remove rice from heat. Leave to stand, covered, until all the liquid has been absorbed, about 5 minutes.

9. Stir in the parsley and the pepper and serve with the cooked veal chops. Spoon the juices from the frying pan over the chops.

Cook's Notes

TIME: Preparation takes about 10 minutes and cooking about 30-40 minutes.

VARIATION: Pork fillets would be a good substitute for the veal chops.

WATCHPOINT: For a milder flavour, use only one stock cube.

STIR-FRY LAMB

SERVES 4

Try this stir-fry with a difference – a dish to be enjoyed all year round.

8 lamb cutlets
Salt and pepper
Knob of butter
1 tbsp vegetable oil
1 large onion, chopped
1 large carrot, diced
½ green pepper, seeded and sliced
½ red pepper, seeded and sliced
50g/2oz button mushrooms, sliced
1 x 100g/4oz can pineapple rings in natural juice
1 tbsp soy sauce
1 x 227g/8oz can Uncle Ben's 3 Minute Long grain rice
225g/8oz bean sprouts

1. Trim the cutlets. Season lightly and arrange them on a foil-lined grill rack.

STEP 1

2. Grill the cutlets for about 5 minutes on each side, until well browned and cooked through.

3. At the same time, heat the butter and oil in a large frying pan. Add the onion and carrot and fry gently until almost soft. Add the peppers and mushrooms and stir-fry for a few minutes.

4. Drain the pineapple, reserving 2 tbsps of the juice, and chop the flesh roughly. Add it to the pan with the soy sauce, seasoning and reserved pineapple juice. Cook for 1 minute.

STEP 3

5. In a separate pan, cook the rice according to the instructions on the can. Add the rice to the other vegetables, stirring well to blend thoroughly.

STEP 5

6. Stir the bean sprouts into the vegetable and rice mixture and cook for about 1 minute, stirring continuously.

7. Serve the grilled cutlets with the stir-fried rice mixture.

Cook's Notes

TIME: Preparation takes about 15-20 minutes. Cooking takes 20-25 minutes.

VARIATION: Peach slices could be used instead of the pineapple rings. The dish could also be made using a 227g/8oz can Uncle Ben's Wholegrain 3 Minute rice.

SURPRISE BURGERS

SERVES 6

Ideal for a children's tea party, or even an adults' barbecue, these exciting burgers will always be in demand.

225g/8oz Uncle Ben's Long grain rice
1kg/2lbs finely minced steak
2 eggs
25g/1oz soft white breadcrumbs
1 tsp salt
Freshly ground pepper

Suggested Fillings
6 slices Cheddar cheese, spread with mustard, or
    fruit chutney
6 thin slices onion, spread with chilli sauce
6 slices tomato, spread with mayonnaise and
    sprinkled with Chopped chives
6 slices ham, spread with French mustard
Sliced dill pickles
Horseradish relish

1. Cook the rice, according to the instructions on the packet.

2. Combine the minced steak, eggs, breadcrumbs and seasonings in a bowl and mix together thoroughly.

STEP 2

3. With lightly floured hands, shape the mixture into twelve thin patties.

STEP 3

4. Place chosen filling on six of the patties.

5. Top with remaining six patties and press edges together firmly.

STEP 5

6. Barbecue over hot coals for approximately 8-10 minutes on each side, or until cooked. Serve with the rice.

Cook's Notes

🕐 TIME: Preparation takes about 15 minutes. Cooking takes 35-40 minutes.

◣ PREPARATION: The burgers can also be cooked under a medium grill or fried gently, with a little fat, to prevent sticking.

❗ WATCHPOINT: If stacking uncooked burgers, interleave with greaseproof paper, to prevent sticking.

DUCK STIR-FRY

SERVES 4

Why not entertain Chinese-style this weekend? This exotic meal will prompt many a well-deserved compliment.

225g/8oz Uncle Ben's Wholegrain rice
4 duck breast fillets
1 onion, sliced
1 clove garlic, crushed
4 sticks celery, cut into 2.5cm/1 inch strips
4 carrots, cut into 2.5cm/1 inch strips
2 large courgettes, topped and tailed and cut into thin strips
100g/4oz cashew nuts
100g/4oz button mushrooms, wiped and halved
1 tbsp soy sauce or 1 tbsp dry sherry
Small can baby sweetcorn, drained
Salt and freshly ground black pepper

---

1. Cook the rice, according to the instructions on the packet. Drain.

2. Skin the duck breasts carefully, with a sharp knife, and put skin to one side.

STEP 2

3. Cut the duck meat into thin strips.

STEP 3

4. Fry duck skin in a wok, or heavy-based frying pan, for 4-5 minutes. Discard skin.

5. Add the onion and garlic to the wok, or pan, and stir-fry for 2 minutes.

6. Add the carrots, courgettes and celery and cook for a further 2 minutes.

7. Add the duck and the nuts and stir-fry for a further 4-5 minutes, or until duck is cooked.

STEP 7

8. 1 minute before end of cooking, add the baby sweetcorn and the mushrooms and 1 tbsp soy sauce, or dry sherry, and season.

9. Serve on a bed of rice.

Cook's Notes

🔥 TIME: Preparation takes about 20-30 minutes. Cooking takes about 15 minutes.

◆ PREPARATION: Begin cooking the rice about 5 minutes before starting to stir-fry, so it will all be ready together.

◯ SERVING IDEAS: Serve with extra soy sauce, to taste.

CURRIED RICE WITH CHICKEN AND ORANGE

SERVES 6

The variations on curry are innumerable – try this interesting blend of oranges and yogurt.

100g/4oz Uncle Ben's Long grain rice
750ml/1¼ pints water
Salt and pepper
1½ tbsps curry powder
2 medium oranges
340g/12oz cooked chicken, cut into bite-sized
    pieces
1 x 400g/14oz can chick peas, drained
75g/3oz sultanas
200ml/7 fl oz natural yogurt

1. Bring the water to the boil in a saucepan, stir in the rice, salt and curry powder, cover the pan and simmer for 20 minutes. Drain and leave to cool.

2. Grate the rind from the oranges and put to one side.

STEP 2

3. Remove remaining pith from the oranges. Dispose of the pith. Using a sharp knife, cut the orange segments away carefully from the inner membranes.

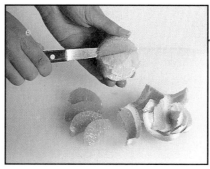

STEP 3

4. Mix the orange segments with the rice, chicken, chick peas and sultanas.

5. Mix the yogurt with the orange rind and season with pepper. Pour this over the rice mixture and stir well.

STEP 5

Cook's Notes

TIME: The rice takes about 20 minutes to cook and then requires about 2 hours to cool. The remaining preparation takes about 20 minutes.

SERVING IDEAS: This a suitable buffet dish, but is also ideal for picnics.

VARIATION: Turkey would be ideal for this dish, in place of the chicken, making it a useful recipe for using up Christmas leftovers.

PREPARATION: To remove pith, and peel, from an orange, hold it upright, with a fork through its centre, and cut downwards from top to bottom with a small, sharp knife.

CHICKEN WITH GRAPES AND MILD CURRY SAUCE

SERVES 4-6

If you're not too sure about hot and spicy food, this mild curry, with its delicate flavour, will change your mind.

225g/8oz Uncle Ben's Long grain rice
1 x 1.6kg/3 1/2lb chicken, cooked
25g/1oz butter, or margarine
1 1/2 tbsps flour
1 tbsp mild curry powder
Large pinch saffron, or turmeric
150ml/ 1/4 pint single cream
Salt and pepper
225g/8oz green seedless grapes, halved
Toasted, flaked almonds, to garnish
Paprika pepper

1. Cook the rice, according to the instructions on the packet. Drain and set aside.

2. Meanwhile, remove bones from chicken and divide the meat into convenient, bite-sized pieces.

STEP 2

3. Simmer the chicken bones gently for 20 minutes with salt, pepper and enough water to make up 200ml/7 fl oz of stock, or use 200ml/ 7 fl oz water and 1 chicken stock cube.

4. In a pan, melt the butter and stir in the flour and the spices. Add the stock gradually and then cook gently, stirring continuously, until the sauce comes to the boil, cooking until thickened.

STEP 4

5. Stir the chicken and cream into the sauce and cook, without boiling, until thoroughly heated through.

6. Add the grapes and season with salt and pepper.

STEP 6

7. Serve on a large plate, surrounded by rice and sprinkled with paprika pepper. Garnish with toasted, flaked almonds.

Cook's Notes

TIME: Preparation takes about 10 minutes. Cooking takes about 30-40 minutes.

VARIATION: Although this dish is designed to be served hot, it could be served cold as part of a summer buffet. Black grapes could be used, if green ones were not available.

CORONATION CHICKEN

SERVES 4

Celebrate Sunday in style with this sumptuous, classic dish.

225g/8oz Uncle Ben's Wholegrain rice, cooked
and cooled
1 x 1.6kg/3½lb chicken, cooked and cooled

Sauce
300ml/½ pint mayonnaise
1 tbsp curry paste
2 tbsps sieved apricot jam
A little single cream
1 red pepper, seeded and sliced, to garnish

1. Slice the chicken into bite-sized pieces.

STEP 1

2. Arrange the chicken pieces over a bed of rice on a serving dish.

3. Mix the sauce ingredients together well and spoon half the sauce over the chicken. Garnish with red pepper.

STEP 3

4. Serve the rest of the sauce separately.

Cook's Notes

TIME: Once the chicken and the rice have been cooked, assembling the dish, including making the sauce, will take about 10-15 minutes. Chilling time is at least half an hour.

VARIATION: If single cream is not available, use a little whole milk to thin down the mayonnaise.

SERVING IDEAS: This dish is ideal for a summer dinner party, or as part of a buffet.

DUCK WITH ORANGE AND ALMOND RICE

SERVES 4

This exquisite meal, with orange and almond rice to complement the flavour of the duck, is designed to suit the most discerning of palates.

25g/1oz unsalted butter
4 duck breast fillets, skinned
1-2 tbsps redcurrant jelly
Rind and juice of 1 orange
Salt and freshly ground black pepper

Orange and Almond Rice
1 tbsp vegetable oil
1 small onion, finely chopped
225g/8oz Uncle Ben's Long grain rice
1 tsp turmeric
1 tsp salt
600ml/1 pint water
Rind of one orange
Freshly ground pepper
15g/½oz butter
Juice of two oranges
50g/2oz toasted almonds
1 tbsp freshly chopped chives or parsley

1. Melt butter in a large frying pan and fry the duck breasts gently for 10-12 minutes on each side. Remove from the pan.

STEP 1

2. Cut 3 long slashes lengthways through each fillet, leaving 2.5cm/1 inch intact at one end. Fan each fillet out and keep hot.

STEP 2

3. In a saucepan, heat the redcurrant jelly and orange juice and rind together slowly, over a gentle heat. Bring to the boil, then spoon over each duck fillet.

4. Garnish with orange rind and serve on a bed of freshly cooked orange and almond rice (see below).

5. To make the orange and almond rice, measure the oil into a medium-sized saucepan. Add the onion and sauté gently, until soft.

6. Add the rice and stir into the onion. Stir in the turmeric, add the water and salt and finely grate the orange rind directly into the mixture. Season with freshly ground black pepper.

7. Bring to a simmer, stirring continuously, then cover with the pan lid and leave on the lowest heat for 20 minutes, or until the rice is tender and all the liquid has been absorbed.

8. Remove the saucepan of rice from the heat. Add the butter, orange juice, toasted almonds and chopped chives, or parsley, to the rice and mix well with a fork. Serve as Step 4, above.

Cook's Notes

🕐 TIME: The duck takes about 30 minutes to cook, including making the sauce. The rice also takes about 30 minutes and should be cooked simultaneously, if possible.

❗ WATCHPOINT: Cover the duck, whilst keeping it hot, to prevent the meat drying out.

SALMON MOUSSE

SERVES 6

Treat yourself and your friends to this delicious and indulgent starter, with its smooth and creamy texture.

75g/3oz Uncle Ben's Long grain rice
1 x 225g/8oz tin salmon
15g/¹⁄₂oz gelatine, dissolved in 2 tbsps hot water
1 tbsp lemon juice
150ml/¹⁄₄ pint mayonnaise
150ml/¹⁄₄ pint double cream, whipped to soft
    peak stage
Salt and pepper
Cucumber slices and lemon twists, or fresh dill,
    to garnish

1. Cook rice, according to the instructions on the packet. Drain and leave to cool.

2. Remove skin and bones from tinned salmon. Mash the salmon to a fine pulp and mix with the rice, lemon juice, mayonnaise, cream and the gelatine. Season to taste.

STEP 2

STEP 2

3. Decorate the bottom of a plain mould with cucumber slices. Pour in the salmon mixture and put into the refrigerator to set.

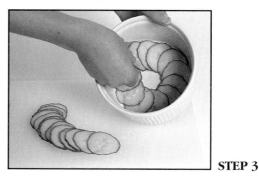

STEP 3

4. Turn out the set mousse, decorate with lemon twists, or fresh dill, and serve chilled with brown bread and butter, or toast.

Cook's Notes

⏱ TIME: Preparation takes about 10 minutes, not including cooking and cooling time for the rice. Allow 2-3 hours for the mousse to set and chill.

❓ VARIATION: Either red or pink salmon is suitable, according to your budget. You could serve the mousse as a main course, with a salad.

❗ WATCHPOINT: Dissolve gelatine gently by adding to cold water, in a cup, putting the cup into a bowl of hot water and stirring, until the gelatine has dissolved. Do not overwhip the double cream.

PAELLA

SERVES 6

With the wide variety of foods available in today's shops, you don't even need to be on the Costa del Sol, to enjoy this typically Spanish speciality.

4 tbsps vegetable oil
1 large onion, chopped
2 cloves garlic, crushed
340g/12oz Uncle Ben's Long grain rice
850ml/1½ pints chicken stock
1 tsp turmeric
Salt
225g/8oz cooked chicken, boned and diced
2 sausages, cooked and sliced
50g/2oz cooked ham, diced
50g/2oz peeled prawns
50g/2oz peas, cooked
½ green pepper, seeded and chopped
½ red pepper, seeded and chopped
2 tomatoes, skinned and sliced
1 small glass dry white wine
Whole prawns and cooked mussels, to garnish

1. Heat oil in a large pan, add the onion, garlic and peppers and fry gently, until soft.

2. Add the rice and fry for 2-3 minutes.

STEP 2

3. Pour in the chicken stock, bring to the boil and stir in the turmeric and salt.

4. Simmer gently for 20 minutes, until the rice is cooked and the stock has been absorbed.

STEP 4

5. Stir the remaining ingredients into the rice just before serving, to heat through.

STEP 5

6. Garnish with the unshelled prawns and cooked mussels.

Cook's Notes

TIME: Preparation takes about 30 minutes. Cooking takes about 25 minutes.

VARIATION: Use a spicy German sausage, for a stronger flavour, or a smoked Danish sausage, for a milder one.

SALMON AND RICE COCOTTES

SERVES 4

Quick and easy to make, these tasty cocottes can be served as impressive starters.

1 x 227g/8oz can Uncles Ben's 3 Minute Wholegrain rice
100ml/31/2 fl oz water
1 x 198g/7oz can salmon, or tuna, drained and flaked
3 spring onions, trimmed and chopped
Pinch of paprika pepper
Salt and pepper
4 eggs
Chopped fresh parsley and paprika pepper, to garnish

1. Preheat oven to 180°C/350°F/Gas Mark 4.

2. Pour water into a saucepan, bring to the boil and add the rice. Cover and simmer for 3 minutes.

3. Stir in the salmon, or tuna, spring onions, paprika and seasoning, to taste.

4. Divide mixture equally between 4 individual, ovenproof dishes and make a well in the centre

STEP 4

5. Break each egg into a cup, or small jug, before pouring carefully into a well. Stand dishes in a roasting tin.

STEP 5

6. Pour enough boiling water into the tin to come halfway up the sides of the dishes. Cover the tin with foil.

STEP 6

7. Bake for 10-12 minutes, or until eggs are cooked to your liking. Serve, garnished with chopped fresh parsley and a sprinkling of paprika pepper.

Cook's Notes

TIME: Preparation takes about 15 minutes. Cooking takes 10-12 minutes.

VARIATION: Use peeled and chopped shallots, as a substitute for the spring onions. In place of the wholegrain rice, you could use long grain rice.

TRAVELLER'S FISH PIE

SERVES 4

You don't really need to be a traveller to sample the delights of this hearty dish - you just need a healthy appetite!

175g/6oz Uncle Ben's Long grain rice
1 tbsp vegetable oil
1 onion, chopped
1 x 425g/15oz can cream of mushroom soup
1 x 195g/7oz tin tuna fish, flaked
4 hard-boiled eggs, sliced
50g/2oz fresh breadcrumbs
50g/2oz Cheddar cheese, grated
25g/1oz butter
Slices of hard-boiled egg and chopped parsley,
    to garnish

1. Cook the rice, according to the instructions on the packet. Drain and keep warm.

2. Heat the oil and fry the onion gently until soft. Add the soup and bring to the boil. Stir the tuna in gently and season to taste.

STEP 2

3. Pour the tuna mixture into a shallow, ovenproof dish and arrange the eggs on top. cover with the rice, then sprinkle over the breadcrumbs and the cheese. Top with flakes of butter.

STEP 3

STEP 3

4. Place under a preheated grill, until golden.

5. Garnish with parsley and slices of hard-boiled egg. Serve immediately.

Cook's Notes

TIME: The rice takes about 20-25 minutes to cook. Preparation and final grilling of the pie takes about 30 minutes.

SERVING IDEAS: Serve this useful supper dish with a selection of fresh vegetables.

CRAB AND MUSHROOMS AU GRATIN

SERVES 2

This is a perfect, year-round dish, which can be made cost-effectively, whether crab is in season or not.

100g/4oz Uncle Ben's Long grain rice
50g/2oz butter
1 large onion, chopped
100g/4oz mushrooms, sliced
25g/1oz flour
2 tbsps dry sherry
300ml/½ pint milk
Salt and freshly ground black pepper
175g/6oz fresh, or frozen, crabmeat
2 tbsps grated Cheddar cheese
2 tbsps breadcrumbs
Cayenne pepper

1. Cook the rice, according to the instructions on the packet. Drain, fluff up with a fork and arrange in a serving dish.

STEP 1

2. While rice is cooking, preheat the grill to hot.

3. Melt the butter in a heavy-based saucepan, add the onion and cook gently for 5 minutes, to soften.

4. Add the sliced mushrooms and stir, until coated with the butter. Cook for a further 5 minutes over a gentle heat.

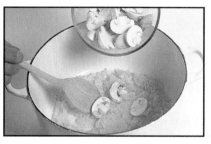

STEP 4

5. Stir the flour into the butter and cook for another minute. Add the sherry and then, gradually, the milk, stirring all the time, until you have a smooth sauce. Season with salt and pepper and cook gently for another 5 minutes.

6. Spread the crabmeat evenly over the rice. Pour the mushroom and onion sauce over the crab.

STEP 6

7. Mix the grated cheese and breadcrumbs with a pinch of cayenne pepper. Sprinkle this breadcrumb mixture over the top of the crab.

8. Grill for 5 minutes, until the surface is golden and bubbling, and serve immediately.

Cook's Notes

TIME: The rice takes 20-25 minutes to cook. Preparation takes about 15 minutes. Cooking takes about 20-25 minutes.

PREPARATION: Whether fresh or frozen, use prepared crabmeat; a mixture of brown and white meat is best.

SERVING IDEAS: This dish is ideal as a substantial starter to a light, cold main course.

RICE RATATOUILLE

SERVES 6

An unusual variation on the traditional ratatouille, the addition of wholegrain rice converts it into a nutritious and filling meal.

225g/8oz Uncle Ben's Wholegrain rice
1 onion, chopped
1 clove garlic, crushed
3 courgettes, sliced
1 aubergine, sliced
6 tomatoes, skinned and chopped
1 green pepper, seeded and finely chopped
1 red pepper, seeded and finely chopped
225g/8oz mushrooms, sliced
Pinch each of marjoram and basil
2 tbsps tomato purée
3 glasses red wine
275ml/½ pint vegetable stock
1 tbsp vegetable oil
50g/2oz wholemeal breadcrumbs
50g/2oz walnuts, chopped

1. Cook the rice, according to the instructions on the packet. Drain, put in a serving dish and keep warm.

2. Meanwhile, heat a little oil in a pan and fry the onion and garlic, until tender.

STEP 2

3. Add the courgettes, aubergine, tomatoes, peppers, mushrooms, marjoram, basil, tomato purée, red wine and stock. Season to taste and simmer for 15 minutes.

STEP 3

4. Pour the ratatouille over the rice.

5. Combine the oil, breadcrumbs and walnuts and sprinkle over the ratatouille. Place under a hot grill, until golden. Serve immediately.

STEP 5

Cook's Notes

TIME: Preparation takes about 15 minutes. If the rice and ratatouille are cooked simultaneously, cooking takes about 30 minutes.

VARIATION: Cooking wine and chicken stock are suitable substitutes for the red wine and vegetable stock respectively.

SERVING IDEAS: Although this dish is a meal in itself, any grilled or roasted lean meat could also be served with it.

SPICY STUFFED MUSHROOMS

SERVES 2-4

The piquant taste of these delightful vegetables makes them ideal either as a starter for four, or as a main meal for two.

2 tbsps vegetable oil
2 small onions, chopped
2 small courgettes, finely chopped
½ tsp ground coriander
½ tsp ground cumin
¼ tsp turmeric
Pinch chilli powder
100g/4oz Uncle Ben's Wholegrain rice
340ml/12 fl oz vegetable stock
Salt and pepper
4 large, flat mushrooms, stalks removed
Shredded Chinese leaves, to serve
25g/1oz cashew nuts, chopped

1. Heat half of the oil in a small pan. Add the onion, courgette and spices and fry gently for 3-4 minutes.

STEP 1

2. Stir in the rice and stock, season and bring to the boil. Cover the pan and simmer for 15 minutes.

3. When the rice is nearly cooked, heat the remaining oil in a frying pan and fry the whole mushrooms and shredded Chinese leaves gently for 2-3 minutes.

STEP 3

4. Turn the Chinese leaves onto a serving plate and place the mushrooms on top.

5. Add the nuts to the cooked rice and pile into the mushrooms, to serve.

Cook's Notes

⏱ TIME: Preparation takes about 10 minutes. Cooking takes about 25 minutes.

◣ PREPARATION: Chinese leaves can be left raw, if a crunchier texture is preferred.

❓ VARIATION: Substitute 1 tsp curry powder for the cumin, coriander and turmeric.

STUFFED AUBERGINES

SERVES 4

Stuffed vegetables are becoming increasingly popular, but the distinct flavour of this dish makes it a perennial favourite.

2 x 200g/7oz aubergines
1 tbsp salt
2 tbsps vegetable oil
1 onion, chopped
100g/4oz Uncle Ben's Long grain rice
1 x 425g/15oz tin tomatoes, roughly chopped
300ml/½ pint stock, boiling
Salt and freshly ground black pepper
50g/2oz cheese, grated

1. Cut the aubergines in half, lengthways. With a sharp knife, score deep slits in the cut surface of each aubergine. Sprinkle the salt over the scored surface and set aside for 30 minutes, to disgorge.

2. Rinse the aubergine halves in plenty of cold water, to remove the salt. Using a serrated knife, remove the flesh from the aubergines, taking care to leave a 0.5cm/¼ inch border of flesh, to form a shell.

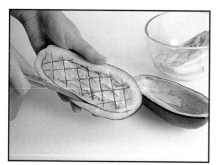

STEP 2

3. Brush the insides of the shells with half the oil. Place the shells in an ovenproof dish and cover with aluminium foil. Bake in a preheated oven, 180°C/350°F/Gas Mark 4, for 30 minutes.

4. Meanwhile, heat the remaining oil in a large saucepan. Add the onion and cook gently for 3 minutes.

5. Chop the aubergine flesh into small pieces and stir this into the cooked onion. Stir-fry for a further minute.

6. Stir the rice, chopped tomatoes and stock into the aubergine mixture. Bring to the boil, then reduce the heat, cover the pan and simmer for 15 minutes, stirring occasionally, until all the liquid has been absorbed. Season to taste.

7. Remove the baked aubergine shells from the oven. Increase the oven temperature to 200°C/400°F/Gas Mark 6. Divide the rice filling equally between each shell, packing the mixture down quite firmly. Sprinkle one quarter of the cheese over each filled aubergine half.

STEP 7

8. Return the aubergines, uncovered, to the oven and cook for 25 minutes, until the cheese is golden brown.

Cook's Notes

TIME: Preparation takes about 40 minutes. Cooking takes about 1 hour.

VARIATION: Home-made chicken or beef stock is preferable, but stock cubes can be used and will give a stronger flavour.

STUFFED HUNGARIAN CABBAGE

SERVES 4

Cabbage with a difference, this delicious mid-European dish is slowly establishing itself here. Easy to cook, it makes a great winter meal.

8 large, whole cabbage leaves, Primo or Savoy
  varieties are best
2 tbsps vegetable oil
1 medium onion, chopped
1 clove garlic, crushed
100g/4oz Uncle Ben's Wholegrain rice
1 red pepper, seeded and chopped
50g/2oz sunflower seeds
50g/2oz sultanas
½ tsp dried thyme
½ tsp dried dill
2 tsps paprika pepper
Salt
350ml/12 fl oz + 4 tbsps water
300ml/½ pint soured cream

1. Plunge the cabbage leaves into a large saucepan of boiling water and cook for 3 minutes, to blanch. Drain the leaves and run them gently under cold water. Shake off excess moisture and, using a sharp knife, trim and discard any thick stalks. Set the leaves aside.

STEP 1

2. Heat the oil in a large saucepan. Fry the onion and garlic gently, until soft, but not browned.

3. Stir all the remaining ingredients, except for the 4 tbsps of water and the soured cream, into the onion and garlic. Bring the mixture to the boil and simmer, uncovered, for 30 minutes, or until the rice is cooked and all the water has been absorbed.

4. Check the seasoning and add a little more paprika pepper and salt, if required.

5. Place an equal amount of the rice mixture in the centre of each cabbage leaf. One at a time, fold the sides of each leaf carefully over the filling. Roll the leaves up into neat bundles and place them into a greased baking dish.

STEP 5

6. Sprinkle the remaining water over the cabbage leaves. Cover the dish with aluminium foil, or a lid, and cook in a preheated oven, 180°C/350°F/Gas Mark 4, for 20 minutes. Serve hot with the soured cream poured over.

STEP 6

Cook's Notes

TIME: Preparation, including cooking the rice, takes about 45 minutes. Final cooking takes about 20 minutes.

PREPARATION: Time the blanching exactly to give best results. The easiest way to blanch vegetables is to lower them into the boiling water in a wire basket, which can then also be lifted out again easily.

SERVING IDEAS: This dish makes a substantial starter. It could also be served as a side dish to a main meat course.

CINNAMON RICE FRITTERS

SERVES 4

This is certainly not a dish for those counting calories, but is nevertheless a mouthwatering recipe.

150g/5oz plain flour
Pinch salt
1 egg, size 2, separated
200ml/8 fl oz milk
50g/2oz Uncle Ben's Long grain rice
4 tbsps caster sugar
Grated rind of one orange
Cinnamon, for dusting
Vegetable oil for deep-frying

---

1. To make the batter, sieve the flour and salt into a mixing bowl. Make a well in the centre and drop in the egg yolk. Using a wooden spoon, work the flour into the egg yolk, adding the milk gradually and beating well after each addition, until a creamy batter is formed. Leave the batter to stand.

STEP 1

2. Cook the rice, according to the instructions on the packet. Drain and stir in half the sugar.

3. Whisk the egg white, until it is stiff, but not dry.

4. Stir the cooked rice and the orange rind into the batter, mixing together well. Using a metal spoon, fold the whisked egg white quickly, but thoroughly, into the rice and batter mixture.

STEP 4

5. Heat the oil in a deep-fat fryer to 180°C/350°F. Drop spoonfuls of the batter mixture into the oil and fry until golden brown. Fry only a few spoonfuls of batter at a time, to prevent the fritters from breaking up or sticking together.

6. Drain the fritters on absorbent kitchen paper and dust with the remaining caster sugar and the cinnamon. Serve piping hot.

STEP 6

Cook's Notes

⏱ TIME: Preparation time is about 30-35 minutes, including cooking the rice.
Cooking the fritters takes about 30 minutes.

◯ SERVING IDEAS: Serve either sauced with a hot fruit purée or accompanied by a

fresh fruit salad, hot or cold.

⚠ WATCHPOINT: It is safest to use a deep-fat fryer with a temperature regulator and safety cutout, to prevent fat overheating.

COURGETTE BAKE

SERVES 4

Not a typical flan, this exciting blend of courgettes, tomatoes and cream is a light and refreshing alternative.

75g/3oz Uncle Ben's Long grain rice
800g/1¾lbs courgettes
4 eggs
200ml/7 fl oz single cream, or milk
Chopped fresh parsley, or fresh mint
Salt and pepper

Tomato Sauce
2 tsps vegetable oil
1 small onion, chopped
450g/1lb tomatoes, skinned, seeded and
    chopped
1 small bunch parsley
Salt and pepper

1. Cook the rice, according to the instructions on the packet. Drain thoroughly and put into a large mixing bowl.

2. Wash and dry the courgettes. Cut them into thin slices.

STEP 2

3. In a small bowl, beat together the eggs and cream.

4. Add the beaten eggs, the courgettes, some chopped parsley, or mint, and seasoning to the rice and mix well. Pour this mixture into a lightly greased 17.5cmx27.5cm/7 inchx11 inch ovenproof dish and bake in a preheated oven, 180°C/350°F/Gas Mark 4, for 55-65 minutes, or until firm.

STEP 4

5. Whilst the dish is cooking, heat the oil in a large frying pan. Fry the onion gently in the hot oil until soft.

6. Liquidise or purée the tomatoes. Stir them into the fried onion, together with the parsley and seasoning. Heat through gently.

STEP 6

7. Serve the courgette bake with the hot tomato sauce.

Cook's Notes

TIME: Preparation takes about 30 minutes, including cooking the rice. Cooking the flan takes about 55-65 minutes.

VARIATION: Add a lightly sautéed, chopped red pepper to the tomato sauce, or spice it up with a little Tabasco sauce.

PREPARATION: Chop the parsley very finely, before adding to the sauce.

SPECIAL FRIED RICE

SERVES 4

A light and fluffy accompaniment to most Chinese meals, this recipe will have your guests asking for more!

225g/8oz Uncle Ben's Long grain rice
2 eggs
15g/½ oz butter, or margarine
1 medium onion, chopped
4 mushrooms, sliced
2 tbsps vegetable oil
50g/2oz cooked ham, or bacon, diced
50g/2oz peeled shrimps
1 tbsp soy sauce
Spring onions and radishes, to garnish

1. Boil rice according to the instructions on the packet.

2. Meanwhile, beat the eggs, until light and fluffy.

STEP 2

3. Melt the butter in a frying pan and add the egg. Cook, until the underside is golden brown. Turn egg mixture over and cook other side, until golden brown.

STEP 3

4. Remove from the pan and chop roughly. Put to one side.

STEP 4

5. In a large pan, fry the the onion and the mushrooms in the oil, until soft.

6. Add all the remaining ingredients to the onion, including the cooked rice and soy sauce. Stir-fry for 5 minutes, until heated through.

STEP 6

7. Garnish with spring onions and radishes and serve immediately.

Cook's Notes

↺ TIME: Preparation takes about 10 minutes. Cooking takes about 30 minutes, including cooking the rice.

◆ PREPARATION: This dish can be cooked in a wok or a frying pan.

? VARIATION: Wholegrain rice could be used as the basis for this dish.

RICE CREAM CRUNCH

SERVES 6

Naughty but nice – a little self-indulgence doesn't harm!

75g/3oz Uncle Ben's Long grain rice
150ml/¼ pint whipping cream
50g/2oz sugar
450g/1lb strawberries, or any soft fruit in season
25g/1oz butter
2 tbsps golden syrup
50g/2oz cornflakes

---

1. Cook rice, according to the instructions on the packet. Drain and leave to cool.

2. Whip cream, until it stands in soft peaks.

STEP 2

3. Fold the rice into the cream and add the sugar.

STEP 3

4. Stir half the strawberries, or other soft fruit, into the rice cream mixture.

5. Melt the butter in a pan and stir in the syrup. Mix well. Add the cornflakes and stir, until thoroughly coated. Leave to cool.

STEP 5

6. Spoon the coated cornflakes over the rice cream mixture. Decorate with the remaining fruit.

Cook's Notes

TIME: Cooking the rice takes 20-25 minutes, plus cooling time. Preparing the rest of the dish takes about 20 minutes.

VARIATION: Use clear honey instead of golden syrup, to coat the cornflakes.

WATCHPOINT: Chill the cream, before whipping, and whip by hand for greater control. Do not overwhip.

PEACH BAVAROIS

SERVES 4-6

This rich and creamy dessert is a perfect delight, especially now that fresh fruit is available all year round.

1litre/1¾ pints milk
75g/3oz Uncle Ben's Long grain rice
6 egg yolks
100g/4oz icing sugar, sifted
A few drops vanilla essence
1 sachet gelatine, soaked in 3 tbsps water
150ml/¼ pint double cream, lightly whipped
15g/½ oz butter
1 x 411g/14½oz can peach slices in syrup, drained

Fruit Purée

450g/1lb strawberries
75g/3oz icing sugar
Juice of 1 lemon

1. Bring 450ml/¾ pint of the milk to the boil, add the rice and simmer for approximately 20 minutes, stirring occasionally, until all the liquid has been absorbed.

2. Meanwhile, whisk together the egg yolks and the sugar, until light and creamy.

STEP 2

3. Scald the remaining milk and add gradually to the eggs. Stir over a gentle heat, until slightly thickened. Add the vanilla essence and the gelatine, stirring without boiling, until dissolved.

4. Pass the custard through a sieve and allow to cool slightly, before mixing with the cooked rice and the lightly whipped cream.

STEP 3

5. Liberally butter a charlotte mould.

6. Pour half the custard and rice mixture into the mould and then arrange the peaches on top. Cover with the remaining mixture and refrigerate overnight.

7. For the fruit purée, wash and hull the strawberries. Liquidise the fruit, sugar and lemon juice in a fruit processor, or push through a sieve.

8. Turn out the mould, when set. Serve with the fruit purée, in a sauce boat or jug.

Cook's Notes

TIME: The bavarois takes about 1 hour to prepare, including cooking the rice, but should be made the day before required, so it can be chilled overnight.

PREPARATION: To help dissolve the gelatine, put into a cup with the cold water and place the cup into a small pan of hot water and stir until dissolved.

VARIATION: Raspberries could be used in the purée, instead of strawberries, or in the bavarois, instead of peaches.

INDEX